Fait

FOUR WEEK MINI BIBLE STUDY

Heather Bixler

Becoming Press, LLC

Heather Bixler/Becoming Press, LLC
www.becomingpress.com

Ordering Information:
Quantity sales. Special discounts are available on quantity purchases by corporations, associations, and others. For details, contact the "Special Sales Department" at website above.

Faith - Four Week Mini Bible Study/Heather Bixler—2nd ed.
ISBN-13: 978-0983468530
ISBN-10: 0983468532

Scripture quotations are from The World English Bible.

Table of Contents

Introduction

He said to them, "Because of your unbelief. For most certainly I tell you, if you have faith as a grain of mustard seed, you will tell this mountain, 'Move from here to there,' and it will move; and nothing will be impossible for you. - **Matthew 17:20**

As I write this Bible Study, it is becoming more apparent to me faith is a choice. Often, we don't walk in faith with God because we don't want to give up control of our life or do not believe God will come through for us or He isn't sovereign.

Before we can experience God's extraordinary grace in our life, we need to choose to believe in Him. We need to trust and know in our hearts that He is sovereign and that the Creator of the universe cannot be held back by anyone or anything. Lack of faith can cause a lot of pain and grief in our life. There are no certainties when it comes to tomorrow. However, there is always faith. Faith in Who God is, What He has already done for us, and His heart for us and humanity as a whole. It takes faith to believe in a Sovereign God.

Our faith begins with what we know and believe about God. Our faith will carry us as far as we are willing to let it take us. Faith is a choice, and we need to begin by choosing to believe in Jesus and His power to move mountains, heal the sick, and save us from all our sins through His sacrifice on the cross.

When we believe in God, we then learn to walk in faith and trust God. First, we must believe. It's up to us; we can either choose to believe in Him or not. But faith will mean nothing until we believe with all our heart that God is who He says He is.

About Faith, Hope, and Love

But now faith, hope, and love remain--these three. The greatest of these is love.
- 1 Corinthians 13:13

This book is the first book in a four-week mini Bible Study series I did on 1 Corinthians 13:13. Over the past three years, God has taken me on a journey to shift my perspective to eternity. We can get so bogged down with the circumstances we face in life.

Every day that I wake up, I can't help but think why I was so fortunate to wake up and be alive TODAY!

When our heart is set on eternity, we learn to live for today, and we are never hesitant to be all that God created us to be.

Why faith, hope, and love? Because these three things will go on forever — this is what we need to focus on today.

Everything else will crumble, but your faith, hope, and love will go on for all eternity. That is the message you will find in this four-week mini-Bible study series. You can learn more about these Bible Studies and the author at www.BecomingPress.com.

Focus on Today

while it is said, "Today if you will hear his voice, don't harden your hearts, as in the rebellion." - **Hebrews 3:15**

Often our heart and mind can wander to the worries and desires of tomorrow. Focusing on today helps us to realize the blessings we have. When our mind and spirit wander to tomorrow or next week, we lose sight of the beautiful things God has already given us.

As it shows in Matthew 6:30, today is the guarantee; tomorrow is not. Today is where we will find His blessings and grace. Has God clothed you, is there food on the table, and do you have a roof over your head today?

If we are going to live by faith, we sometimes need to make our decisions based on today. How would your choices differ if they were rooted in the here and now, today?

If we live by faith, then we need to learn how to become TODAY seed planters. When we focus on the big picture, our hearts become overwhelmed. The power of walking in faith is having enough faith in God to get through today. When we focus on today, we begin to plant the seeds of tomorrow, and we will reap a harvest.

It takes faith to move our focus off tomorrow and back to today. But it's the first step in getting our life back in line with walking in God's will because the only way to walk in His will is to walk in faith.

> Thou shalt therefore obey the voice of the LORD thy God, and do his commandments and his statutes which I command thee this day. - **Deuteronomy 27:10**

Focusing on today doesn't mean we sit idly by. We need to plant the seeds of tomorrow, today. Focusing on today means we are not going to plant the seeds of today based on the harvest we have yet to receive. A farmer can only plant corn seeds if they have corn seeds available to them. Plant the seeds you can plant today!

When we focus on today, we get our hopeful anticipation back. We learn to trust that the blessings will come; our excitement in the surprises of tomorrow fill our heart. Faith in God is not a burden; our faith in Him helps us overcome the struggles we face every day. Our faith in Him will release us from feeling the need to conquer every daily battle on our own. In life and death, our faith in Jesus will carry us on through to Eternity.

Life Application

- What seeds can you plant today?

- Read Matthew 6:19-34. Do you have faith in someone or something other than God?

- What daily actions do you take to control this someone or something?

- If you had faith in God would you need to try to control Him?

Week One Scripture Journal

Week One Memory Verse:
Psalm 40:4

Day One: Write down the scripture you are learning in the space provided below:

Day Two: Write scripture down four times on a sticky note and place them around the house.

Day Three: Look up 3 different versions of scripture. Write them in the space provided below:

Day Four: Write down the memory verse 10x's in space provided below:

Day Five: Read Psalm 40 and journal your thoughts in the space provided below:

Day Six: Write scripture by memory 3x's in the space provided below.

Day Seven: Share your scripture with a friend.

Discussion Questions

The following questions are designed to be used within a group discussion about the scripture you memorized.

1. When we are impatient what are we focusing on? Today or tomorrow?

2. Could we ever fathom or even put together the life God has planned for us? Why do we try to figure it all out?

3. When we point our focus back on God how does that help lead us in the direction God wants us to go?

Focus on Truth

Teach me your way, Yahweh. I will walk in your truth.
Make my heart undivided to fear your name.
- **Psalm 86:11**

Often we lie to our self saying that we are in control or we are capable. But when we live a life where we believe we are capable or have total control, we often live a busy, stressed-out life where our only hope is in ourselves or some other person or thing.

To live a life of faith, we need to acknowledge the truth, and the truth is this: God is the one in control, and He is the one who makes us capable. Focusing on this truth brings us to a place where we live a life surrendered to Him.

When we live a life where we try to control everything, our fear and stress begin to control us and our actions. When we start to put our faith in things like money, which is so unpredictable, we worry.

Realizing that God is in control of everything is the first step of focusing on the truth. The next step is allowing God to have control over your life.

If we want to live a life walking by faith, we need to know that we can't, but God can. He can do anything, or He can do nothing. It is our choice whether or not we will let Him in our life, which determines what He will do in our life. Making this choice to let Him in our life is how we walk in faith, trust in His sovereign will, and surrender our lives to Him.

Life Application

- What do you try to control in your life?

- What do you cling to for your security?

- If God asked you to let this go, would you? Why or why not?

Pray to God and tell Him you can't do it. Tell Him you can't manage it all. Tell Him you are scared. Tell Him to then fill you with His truth.

Week Two Scripture Journal

Week Two Memory Verse:
Ephesians 6:16

Day One: Write down the scripture you are learning in the space provided below:

Day Two: Write scripture down four times on a sticky note and place them around the house.

Day Three: Look up 3 different versions of scripture. Write them in the space provided below:

Day Four: Write down the memory verse 10x's in space provided below:

Day Five: Read Ephesians Chapter 6 and journal your thoughts in the space provided below:

Day Six: Write scripture by memory 3x's in the space provided below.

Day Seven: Share your scripture with a friend.

Discussion Questions

The following questions are designed to be used within a group discussion about the scripture you memorized.

1. How does our faith allow us to stand firm against the Devil?

2. Does our resistance of the Devil come from our own power?

3. What was Paul's request for prayer? Where does his boldness come from? Where can we find the power to be bold in our faith?

WEEK THREE

God Wants Commitment

Commit your way to Yahweh. Trust also in him, and he will do this **- Psalm 37:5**

Definition of commitment: *something pledged* [1]

Often when we walk in faith, we begin to have doubts. When I have these doubts, I begin to consider a new direction I would rather go. My mind begins to wander through all the possibilities of what I could do to make all my dreams come true or resolve all the pain I might be experiencing at that moment.

The test of doubt comes to test our commitment to God and His plan for us. When our mind begins to wander, so does our heart. Our commitment to the Lord depends on our trust and delight in Him.

Commitment to God's will and plan for our life isn't always easy. It's like marriage, sometimes you will

---

[1] "Commitment." Merriam-Webster.com. Merriam-Webster, n.d. Web. 3 Nov. 2017.

have your ups and downs, but through them all, we need to keep our focus and remain committed.

Through our commitment to God's plan and will for our life, we will begin to see the beauty in His blessings. Just like in marriage, if we are to get through the challenging moments, on the other side, we get to experience God's great blessings and His amazing grace.

When we have a heart committed to God and His will for our life, then we are living a life of faith and trust in Him. To be committed to God requires one thing from us: Perseverance to remain committed to Him and what He has us doing. If we know in our heart without any doubt that this is where God has put us, then we need to cling to that truth when the doubt creeps in, and we are ready to break our commitment.

Commitment is an act; it is a promise we have made in our hearts. Sometimes, to remain committed to our spouse in marriage, we need to take "divorce" out of the equation. If we are to stay committed to God's plan for our life, then we need to take our "other plans," and even our dreams and doubts, out of the equation. We need to take our expectations out of the picture and allow God's plan to unfold before our eyes. Anything we plan for our life could never compare to the plans God has for our life. Oh, the beauty that will grow when we remain committed to HIM!

Life Application

- Are you committed to God's will for your life?

- Do you often have a Plan B in case something doesn't go the way you hoped it would?

- Do you struggle with doubt when things seem to be going wrong?

- Do you feel abandoned by God when things don't go according to plan?

Week Three Scripture Journal

Week Three Memory Verse:
James 1:3

Day One: Write down the scripture you are learning in the space provided below:

Day Two: Write scripture down four times on a sticky note and place them around the house.

Day Three: Look up 3 different versions of scripture. Write them in the space provided below:

Day Four: Write down the memory verse 10x's in space provided below:

Day Five: Read James Chapter 1 and journal your thoughts below:

Day Six: Write scripture by memory 3x's in the space provided below:

Day Seven: Share your scripture with a friend.

Discussion Questions

The following questions are designed to be used within a group discussion about the scripture you memorized.

1. What will we have when our endurance is fully developed? How will it be complete?

2. Define waver. Why shouldn't people with wavering commitment expect to receive anything from the Lord? When we waver in our faith, can God rely on us?

3. In James Chapter 1 what does it say divides our faith? What causes your faith to waver?

WEEK FOUR

Faith = Grace

In the fourth watch of the night, Jesus came to them, walking on the sea. When the disciples saw him walking on the sea, they were troubled, saying, "It's a ghost!" and they cried out for fear. But immediately Jesus spoke to them, saying "Cheer up! It is I! Don't be afraid." Peter answered him and said, "Lord, if it is you, command me to come to you on the waters." He said, "Come!" Peter stepped down from the boat, and walked on the waters to come to Jesus. But when he saw that the wind was strong, he was afraid, and beginning to sink, he cried out, saying, "Lord, save me!" Immediately Jesus stretched out his hand, took hold of him, and said to him, "You of little faith, why did you doubt?" When they got up into the boat, the wind ceased. Those who were in the boat came and worshiped him, saying, "You are truly the Son of God!" - **Matthew 14:25-33**

When we read the Bible, we may overlook the simple answers to most of our questions; however, we might struggle to find the answers to our most pressing questions.

If we look closely, we will see that the main ingredient to receiving God's grace and favor is faith. Through our faith, we welcome the grace of God through Jesus' death on the cross. We might seek certainty in our salvation, our eternal destination, and we might want to know that nothing will harm us when we take risks and walk in obedience to what God is calling us to. But when we look for this reassurance, we are often lead to scripture that tells us to have faith and trust in the character of God.

God's grace is always there for us, we need to take hold of it and claim it in our life, but the only way we can do this is to humble ourselves before Him and accept it by faith. There is nothing we can do to earn His favor and grace, and through faith, there will be an overflow of fruit from our walk of obedience to Christ.

When we embrace humility and have faith in God's sovereign will over our life, we learn to accept whatever the outcome may be, and we can let go of our pride and control. We might want to heal and have prayers filled with good things that align with God's promises in His word and His will for all humanity. But are we humble and faithful enough to accept whatever the outcome might be? Are we willing to embrace God's sovereignty?

When we have faith, we continue to walk in His grace which allows us to do the things we cannot and can only do through Him. Through our humility and His grace, God is glorified, and we are made smaller. But this is OK because finally, we are walking with Him and experiencing life as we have never experienced it before.

When we walk in faith and obedience to HIM, we can be confident that whatever we do will be covered in His grace and favor. You see, if we are going to receive His grace, learn to walk in it, and be covered in God's favor, then we need to have faith and let go of our fear.

It was faith that allowed Peter to walk on water, and it was fear that brought him down. It wasn't by Peter's ability that he could walk on water but through God's grace. Peter lacked the power to walk on water when he decided to have fear instead of faith.

When we walk in fear, we are not walking in His grace. If we choose our desires and place them before God, we are taking advantage of His grace.

God's grace is a beautiful thing, and it's all around us. What are you going to do with His grace? Walk-in it, turn your back on it, or take it for granted?

If we are going to walk in under His grace in faith, then we need to let go of our fear and trust that God is who He says He is.

Life Application

- What fears are holding you back from walking in faith? List three things where you have seen God's grace active and present in your life.

- List three reasons why you CAN trust God?

- List three reasons why you don't trust God? Are these things true?

- Do you believe that the healing power of Jesus can be found in the world today? Why or why not?

- What do you believe God can do in your life if you had faith like a mustard seed?

Week Four Scripture Journal

Week Four Memory Verse:
Hebrews 11:6

Day One: Write down the scripture you are learning in the space provided below:

Day Two: Write scripture down four times on a sticky note and place them around the house.

Day Three: Look up 3 different versions of scripture. Write them in the space provided below:

Day Four: Write down the memory verse 10x's in space provided below:

Day Five: Read Hebrews Chapter 11 and journal your thoughts below:

Day Six: Write scripture by memory 3x's in the space provided below:

Day Seven: Share your scripture with a friend.

Discussion Questions

The following questions are designed to be used within a group discussion about the scripture you memorized.

1. What must we believe when we go to God?

2. In all the stories outlined in Hebrews Chapter 11, what was the one thing each person did in order to receive what God had for them?

3. How long did they believe in God and that God would keep His promises?

Hope Foundation

Below is week one of the next Bible Study in this series titled: Hope - Four Week Mini Bible Study! This Bible Study can be purchased online at:

http://becomingpress.com

"Not only this, but we also rejoice in our sufferings, knowing that suffering works perseverance; and perseverance, proven character; and proven character, hope: and hope doesn't disappoint us, because God's love has been poured out into our hearts through the Holy Spirit who was given to us." - **Romans 5:3-5**

It took me a while to get to the point where I stopped praying for God to give me what I wanted, and instead, I started praying for what **He** wanted.

Waiting for my husband to be healed from his disease was depressing. But in my mind, I was clinging to hope that God could, and would, heal my husband.

It took me a while to realize that faith and hope aren't about what you will receive, it is about what you believe.

It takes great faith to trust that no matter what happens, God is still good. When we have that kind of faith, then we have hope in the presence of the Spirit in our life.

Maybe as a society, we have "hope" all wrong. We hope for provision, success, healing, a bigger house, children, and relationships. Our view on hope needs to be changed. We need the light of the truth to be shined on what hope truly is.

Romans 5:3-5 shows us that hope comes through trials. Suffering, perseverance, character, then comes hope. Hope isn't a wish or a dream — hope is a way of thinking, and it's a way of living. Hope is born from the strength and confidence that only comes from the Spirit. That's where hope lives and gives us the motivation to keep pressing forward with a joyful heart.

Hope isn't about waiting for our desires to be fulfilled. Hope is knowing the Holy Spirit and leaning into His presence that is always with us. This is hope...it knows that no matter what, God is good, and He is always with you.

Life Application

"It took me awhile to realize that faith and hope isn't about what you will receive, it is about what you believe."

- Do you think of hope as wanting and waiting for your desires to be manifested in your life?

- What if your desires are not in line with God's will for your life? What if they are?

- Will wishful thinking make God's will happen faster in your life?

- Will anything that is in line with God's sovereign will happen before, or after, He chooses it to happen?

- Can you put your hope in His sovereign will?

- Will you trust in Him and find hope in His presence through anything that may happen in your life?

Week One Scripture Journal

Week One Memory Verse:

Proverbs 24:14.

Day One: Write down the scripture you are learning in the space provided below:

Day Two: Write scripture down four times on a sticky note and place them around the house.

Day Three: Look up 3 different versions of the scripture. Write them in the space provided below:

Day Four: Write down the memory verse 10x's in space provided below:

Day Five: Read Proverbs 24 and journal your thoughts in the space provided below:

Day Six: Write scripture by memory 3x's in the space provided below:

Day Seven: Share your scripture with a friend.

Discussion Questions

The following questions are designed to be used within a group discussion about the scripture you memorized.

- How do you define wisdom? How do you define understanding? Look up these words in the dictionary and discuss the definition.

- Name three foolish behaviors outlined in Proverbs 24. Do you see any of these being displayed in your own life.

- How can these behaviors prevent you from having a mind that is focused on the Spirit? How do they steal your hope?

About the Author

Heather is a mom of three, married to a firefighter, and she is a writer. She is passionate about sharing God's word in a practical and loving way.

He has said to me, "My grace is sufficient for you, for my power is made perfect in weakness." Most gladly therefore I will rather glory in my weaknesses, that the power of Christ may rest on me.-**2 Cor 12:9**

Follow Heather

- **Author Blog:** HeatherBixler.com

- **Facebook:** http://facebook.com/HeatherBixlerWrites

- **Free Bible Studies:** http://biblestudyforher.com

Reviews Needed!

I would love to hear your feedback — please leave your reviews of *Faith - Four Week Mini Bible Study* online wherever books are sold!

More Resources

To view more practical Bible Studies visit:

http://becomingpress.com

Printable Bible Studies:

http://shop.biblestudyforher.com

Lead a small group: Join our online leader guide and receive resources for you to use in your Faith - Four Week Mini Bible Study small group/Bible Study!

Learn more and sign up here:

https://www.becomingpress.com/FaithLeader

Made in the USA
Monee, IL
02 January 2023

23938887R00036